JESU

CHRISTY WIMBER

Edited by Frank A. DeCenso Jr.

DESTINY IMAGE PUBLISHERS

Scripture is the authors' own. Please note that Destiny Image's publishing style capitalizes certain pronouns in Scripture that refer to the Father, Son, and Holy Spirit, and may differ from some publishers' styles. Take note that the name satan and related names are not capitalized. We choose not to acknowledge him, even to the point of violating grammatical rules.

DESTINY IMAGE® PUBLISHERS, INC.

P.O. Box 310, Shippensburg, PA 17257-0310

"Speaking to the Purposes of God for this Generation and for the Generations to Come."

This book and all other Destiny Image, Revival Press, Mercy Place, Fresh Bread, Destiny Image Fiction, and Treasure House books are available at Christian bookstores and distributors worldwide.

For a U.S. bookstore nearest you, call 1-800-722-6774.

For more information on international availability, call 717-532-3040.

Reach us on the Internet at www.destinyimage.com.

Digital Edition ISBN: 978-0-7684-1748-7

Trade Paper ISBN: 978-0-7684-1747 0

Originally published in *Catching God's Heart*, ISBN 978-0-7684-3250-3.

Jesus Chose the Sinners

Christy Wimber

Jesus Chose the Sinners

I think my young son, John, said it best when I asked him, "If Jesus was standing in front of you right now, what do you think He would say to you?"

He didn't even hesitate, saying, "He would say, I am here to protect you, and I will stand up to anybody that would want to hurt you."

I thought, *You know, if we all felt like that, I think it would change the way we approach our Heavenly Father.* If you know your Father is there for you—in a sense, that He has your back—then of course you would tell Him everything. Of course He would be the first One you and I would run too no matter what we're facing.

Intimacy In and Through Us

One of the greatest promises you and I have is that He always sees us not as we are, but as we will and should be. He is your greatest fan; He is the one that will always be faithful to the end of the ages. He is the one that loves you and never ignores you when you cry for help (see Isa. 30:19).

But there's always so much more involved with intimacy than we realize.

Do you feel like God has your back? Do you feel like He is the safest place for you? How you answer those two questions will pretty much tell you how much intimacy you have with the Father.

No true transaction of intimacy takes place between people unless trust is involved. Only when I trust someone am I able to open my heart in a vulnerable and transparent way. Trust is at the core of intimacy with our relationships we have around us in our daily lives, as well as with the Lord.

One way to really know what you trust is to ask yourself the question, "What do I run to when I get great or horrible news?" Do you call a friend?

Your spouse? Do you run to the bar or to the fridge? What you rely on is what you trust in because we're called to trust in Him, and we show we're trusting Him when we're leaning on Him, meaning to find refuge. (See Proverbs 3:5.)

Trust can be such a huge issue for people, but trusting is the key to intimacy. People are dying all around us for the kind of intimacy Jesus desires to have with you and I. And I don't just mean people that aren't saved—I mean people in the church. Too many people know about God—in fact, they even know all the right actions and traditions—yet they don't know Him on a deep, personal level.

Do you know the Father not just by what you do, but from who you are? I think it's important to ask ourselves that question. I know I can do many things for God, and I know it moves His heart to know I love doing His Kingdom work, but I also know that at the end of the day, what my King wants out of me is just that—*me*. He wants intimate relationship with Christy. The King wants you.

I find it interesting how important intimacy is with the Lord, since He created us to have a deep relationship with Him as well as with each other. And, only when we're in touch with the

One who created every aspect of who we are, are we really able to understand who we truly are in Christ and all He has for us.

If I don't really know how God sees me, then how can I extend that offer to others? How can I model that to others, unless there's such a difference in me because I am being touched and seen over and over again by the One who made me? It's when He sees me and I know He sees me, yet I feel safe.

I still believe that at the end of the day He is still the safest place for me—He is my protector. He is the one who will always have my back.

Look at the story of the woman at the well in John 4. It wasn't just that Jesus spoke to her—it was that He saw what everyone else couldn't. He spoke to her heart. He spoke into the heart of who she really was. How many times do you think she walked around town and the people spoke behind her back? How many times do you think she heard the people whisper loudly even though she was present? How many times do you think she felt the stares of judgment all around her?

Jesus cut through all that and told her how it was, but in a way that spoke directly to her heart. Not with judgment, but in a way of seeing the real her.

If Jesus would have spoken to her in a judgmental sort of way, her response would have been much different. Her response would have been more defensive, or she would have said nothing and run.

Yet Jesus saw past the sin to see the sinner, in such an intimate way that spoke directly to her heart. There was a transaction that took place that was so intimate that she was taken aback. Her sin wasn't a "turn-off" to Jesus; He knew who she was and what she was about. In fact, He even knew what others would think of Him because He was speaking to her. Just the fact that they were alone talking could have started more gossip.

Yet it didn't seem to bother Jesus a bit.

And the good news? Our sin isn't a turn-off to Jesus, either! All we have to do is look at the Scriptures and who Jesus had around Him. The people that Jesus picked to carry on the church were so messed up. None of them went to seminary or had great reputations. Most of them were ordinary people that no one else would have picked to come on their team.

But not Jesus. He chose the thief, the tax collector, and the guys that fished for a living. He chose the people that others didn't seem to really acknowledge or particularly like. But when He spoke, it hit them at the core of who they were, so that they were ready to drop everything just to follow this Man. Just to have relationship with this Jesus.

If we look at how Jesus always saw the difference between the person and whatever "sin" they might have done, I think we could catch the very heart of God, not only for ourselves, but also for those around us. I think we get too scared of sin. However, it didn't seem to bother Jesus much; He still chose to talk to, eat with, and fellowship on intimate levels with those that didn't have it all together. And in turn, they were the ones that invited him in—they wanted to be with this Man called Jesus. The invitation is always what moves the heart of Jesus.

In pastoring, I've found too many people don't talk to God much, mostly because of shame. We tend to go to God about surface stuff— what financial need we might have, what we're worried about at the time, what we need some faith for at the time. Yet in Romans it talks about the Holy Spirit needing to intercede on our behalf because most of the time we aren't even in touch with what our real needs are.

True intimacy comes where He sees into who we really are. There's that connection that takes place, that fills a void in us—"our deep calling to His deep" (See Psalms 42:7.)

Too many people are afraid of intimacy because they're afraid of being "found out." I mean, we do that in relationships all the time. Scared to be the real us, feeling that if we do then the person won't really like us or want to be our friend. But true intimacy comes when we share the deepest parts of who we are and the person loves us even more for sharing.

Remember Abraham, who was called "a friend of God"? And really, why was that? They spoke face to face. There were exchanges that took place.

Oftentimes, people think that anyone knowing their heart is too scary.

So, most interaction is the usual, "How are you?"

"Good. And you?" "I'm fine."

"How's work?"

"Good."

"Well, tell your family hello. See you later!"

Doesn't that sound familiar? This sort of surface interaction is how we tend to communicate much of the time.

In my own life I've found it's easy for me in my intimate relationship with others to be too worried about what they can do to hurt me. So, to be vulnerable is to put myself in a place where I can be ruined. It seems like too much of a risk at times. It would be much easier for me just to have my intimacy with the Father, in fact, it would be a lot easier at times! But in order for God to take me to another level of trust, I have to be able to trust those He also sends into my life. It's just part of it.

I've found that in my intimate times with the Lord, He shows me where to go. He shows me those He himself is bringing into my life, and I have a choice whether or not I will trust Him through that process. But every time it seems to take me to a deeper level of trust and intimacy with Him. I know that even if no one sticks by me—even if I am betrayed or hurt in some way—I will still have the Lord.

Spending time with God is never just about us and the Father. It's always for those around us, too. What happens in me—God's Kingdom in me—is what creates His Kingdom around me. Everything I learn from the Father is for a reason. There are things He wants to show me that will only come when it's just He and I.

I mean, look at Jesus, our model of prayer, who went to go be with the Father. It wasn't just to be encouraged and to get filled up again, it was also to know the Father's heart and plan for those Jesus was around. So Jesus knew what the Father's heart was for the people. Remember, Jesus could only do whatever the Father showed Him (see John 5:19).

You and I will not be able to catch God's heart for those around us unless we catch it for ourselves first. We must see the bigger picture as to why He wants to move in us and around us. God cannot do through you what He hasn't done in you first.

See, I think when we talk about intimacy with the Father, we have to be able to catch His heart for others in a way where we are able to get past all the junk in people's lives. Where through you and I we have an intimate encounter with the Lord Himself. Where all we're doing is being the midwife, in a sense. Where we're just part of the transaction, however, we don't feel the need to make it about ourselves, but rather are able to show the people how to connect to the Father. How He really loves and sees who they are, not just what they may have done.

If we don't catch the intimacy the Father has for us, then it's too difficult to be able to see that for others. At the end of the day, I know that many won't be able to see who the person of Christy is, but I do know that my intimacy with the Father is what makes it possible for me to see that for others. It doesn't take a genius or a prophetic gifting to see what's wrong with people. However, it takes some real courage, effort, and risk to be able to see people the way Christ does.

People don't need us; they need the God in us. You can never overestimate the power of your intimacy with Christ. Never is it a waste of time, and never is it just for us.

One thing I've learned throughout the years is for me, the safest place is my time just between God and me. How He uses that is up to Him. But I know that every time I'm with Him, He causes me to see things the way He does. He gives me His heart for people, and without intimacy it would be impossible.

I really love being around people at times that have no idea of who God is. I love it that they don't know how to talk, walk, or dress "Christianese." It doesn't bother me a bit. I mean, how do they know unless someone reaches out to share and be another option?

My husband and I were at his work party not long ago, which was quite interesting but we had a great time. But why we had such a great time is that we got to hang out with people that don't know the Lord yet. One guy walked up to us and said, "Now I know you're religious, so forgive me for my *%^%#* language."

So I said to him, "Well, I'm not religious, but I am a pastor."

And this guy just looked at me with the funniest face and responded by saying, "Well, how the heck do you do that?"

I love people's responses to something nonreligious. I think it's so great to see people around us get an encouraging message that doesn't have to do with something they may be doing wrong with their life. In fact, I think it's important as believers that we're out offering the same message that someone went out of their way to offer to us.

One of the most powerful witnessing tools for me is hearing the Father's heart for someone I'm talking to. Asking the question, "Lord, what would You like to say to this person today?" People aren't expecting some encouraging word for nothing, and in my opinion the gift of encouragement is the most under-used spiritual gift! And the amazing thing is, anyone can do it!

Just like you and I need to know we're OK. Just like you and I need to be encouraged—how much more do the people around you need it? The ones that have no other hope than what they can find in themselves.

See your ability to open up to the Father. To catch His heart for you is what He's after. But in those times of intimacy with Him, He will begin to show you things for those around you that will not only change their lives, but it will take you to a deeper level of your walk with Jesus.

Surrender your heart to Jesus in a way that you're learning to "find refuge" in Him, trusting Him with all you are. Learn to trust Him in a way that you know He is the safest place to be. That when all is said and done, without hesitation, you know God has your back. That He is your great Protector!

About Christy Wimber

Christy Wimber, John and Carol Wimber's daughter-in-law, has been involved with the Vineyard Movement since the beginning. She worked for years at Vineyard Ministries and Vineyard Music. She and her husband, Sean, oversee Doin' the Stuff (DTS), which handles John Wimber materials as well as others in the Vineyard Movement. Christy and Carol released a DVD, "Back to our Roots," which covers the history of the Vineyard Movement. She has also released a book collecting John Wimber's teachings, The Way In Is the Way On. She teaches at conferences and retreats worldwide.

Destiny Image Books by Christy Wimber

The Power of His Presence

NOTES

Printed in Poland
by Amazon Fulfillment
Poland Sp. z o.o., Wrocław

50335702R00022